Hard Hitting Lessons

Some not-so-obvious business lessons learned from playing football

by Jim Tabaczynski

"You can learn more character on the two-yard line than anywhere else in life."

Paul Dietzel,
Head Football Coach
Louisiana State University

Table on Contents

Preface i
Overview viii
One Good Turn 1
Know Your Stuff 5
Marching Orders 16
No Man is an Island 20
Quality Throughout 24
Back to Basics 31
The Post-Game Interview 38
Post Scripts 40
Epilogue 47

Preface

Growing up, my life was a constant cycle of sport. Baseball began in the spring and carried through the end of summer. In the waning days of summer, football began and lasted until almost Thanksgiving just as basketball began. Basketball continued through the winter until spring when, lo and behold, it was time once again for baseball. And the cycle repeated itself year after year.

During my high school days, one by one the sports starting dropping off until only football was left. With a partial college scholarship for football, it became the "money sport." Football was paying the bills so to speak and, as such, demanded all my focus and all my attention. But I was not complaining. Well, not too much.

Lest anyone get the wrong idea, despite how much I loved playing, I was not a great athlete. Not by any stretch of anyone's imagination. My dad told me once after my playing days were through that he was very proud of my meager achievements on the field because he knew I had to work at it. Nothing athletic came easily to me. I was not a natural athlete. Any degree of success I attained was the result of determined struggle. But that was half the fun. I think.

I was just so damned happy to be out there, I didn't care. I guess I fell into the category of the just-put-me-in-coach kind of player. And some of the lessons that I will detail here helped me get the opportunity to get the chance to get in the game.

But it was a struggle. It did not come easily. No sir.

Dropping Like Flies

My days as a player of organized basketball came to a screeching halt when the junior varsity coach in high school told me, "You're a pretty good ball handler. You're not a bad rebounder and you play great defense... but you can't shoot!" So much for basketball.

In baseball, I did have some natural ability. I could pitch. My defense was just average. My hitting was sporadic at best. But I could pitch. I was a sidearmer with a good fastball and a sweeping roundhouse curve that my dad taught me. My dad also taught me what he called a one-finger knuckleball which I threw as a drop pitch. That was something else. I had fun with that one.

Did I have any future in baseball? I don't know if anything would have ever come of it, but I even spoke briefly with a scout from the Cleveland Indians. But that's another story for another day.

My playing days in baseball took a turn when one day I went to warm up before practice and felt a pain in my upper arm, near my shoulder. What happened? Who can say? In those days, players were not rushed off to the nearest sports clinic as they are today. There was no "Tommy John" surgery. Most people familiar with the situation simply shrugged and said, "He threw his arm out." Not much of a medical diagnosis, but it was all the explanation and therapy that one was about to receive.

Did I overextend something? Did I tear something? Your guess is as good as mine. But I could never throw with the same intensity ever again. To this day, if I throw a rock, a football, a baseball or a snowball, I still can feel it.

So much for baseball.

That leaves football. Sometimes I thought that the only reason I played football for as long as I did was that I was too dumb to quit. That could be true. Let's not go there.

In the end, I played football all through college. Being ineligible to play varsity as a freshman – as we all were back then – I broke in as a starter for the third game of my sophomore year and continued to start for the next three years through the conclusion of my senior season. The team enjoyed much more success than I ever did as an individual. The winning made it a lot of fun. For myself, I persevered – toiling away in relative obscurity, and loving every minute of it.

Whenever I've been asked if I would do it again, I unhesitatingly say, "Absolutely. Without a doubt." Even when I think back to working out in the off season, to enduring spring football practice and the hell that was known as summer camp, and even when I look back in disbelief on some of the paces we were put through, I still say, "Absolutely. Without a doubt." In many respects, it was the best time of my life.

Today there are players who back away from the game for health reasons. There are former players who lament their current physical difficulties which they claim were brought on by football. I, however, escaped relatively unscathed. I have a few scars (literally) but nothing catastrophic.

By today's standards (hmmmmm,) I probably had a concussion in high school. After being inadvertently kicked in the head, I blacked out for about a quarter and a half – from early in the third quarter until there were about four minutes left in the game. During that time, we had scored another touchdown and the other team scored one as well. What happened in between? I have no idea – although I did play the entire time. To this day, I don't remember.

Aside from that, my knees ache on occasion and my back bothers me somewhat, but I have experienced relatively few significant health problems. Maybe that's why I don't hesitate to say, "Absolutely. Without a doubt." Maybe. But it was one helluva ride. One that I don't regret. Not for an instant.

And Then There Were None

However, football after college was not a realistic expectation. At the time, my alma mater, Edinboro State College in Pennsylvania, was a small school with a relatively small football program. Of all my college teammates (and to the best of my knowledge of all the players in the Pennsylvania State College Athletic Conference), only one was drafted into the National Football League (and played for four or five years.) Unfortunately (or fortunately) I was among the other 99.99 percent who, when our college playing days were over, we hung up our spikes.

Although I was contacted by a couple of semi-pro teams, that did not seem like a realistic proposition. When asked by a family friend if the NFL draft was in my future, I responded simply, "I only lack three things to make it in professional football — size, speed and strength. Other than that, I'm an ideal candidate."

As Clint Eastwood said in one of the Dirty Harry movies, "A man's got to know his limitations." I was realistic enough to know my limitations and that my playing days were through.

So my days of playing organized sports ended.

My dad's oft-repeated counsel was to play as much and as often as you could growing up, because someday you'll reach a point in your life where you won't be able to play anymore. It had nothing to do with talent or physical ability, but he was wise enough to know that life would get in the way. Family. Kids. Job. Those things tend to take precedence over a ball and a glove. For the most part, he was right. Sport became something that you tried to squeeze in whenever you could.

Nonetheless, over the years, I've tried to remain somewhat active. I've played a little softball. I tried tennis for a while. (Never really warmed up to that.) I played a little handball and a fair amount of racquetball for several years.

I was never a runner – and had no intentions of ever becoming one. That's because we had to run a mile under a prescribed time at the beginning of summer football camp every year in college. That made running as much a mental endurance as it was physical. All summer, as I worked out for football, that Sword of Damocles of *making my mile* hung over me.

> *An aside*: if you didn't make your mile, you were enrolled in the Early Morning Track Club which involved being on the track at 6:00 a.m. everyday during summer camp to run your mile again, until you made your time. And, after running your 6:00 a.m. mile, you then had to endure three-a-day practices.

When they first announced the Early Morning Track Club in the spring of our freshman year, I turned to my roommate and said, "Ain't no way in the world are they getting me up at 6 o'clock in the morning to run any goddamn mile." I made my mile every year. More on that later.

But most of my athletic endeavors through life have focused on golf. Actually golf for me has been similar to football. I love it and I've worked at it but have never really broken through to a point where I could lay claim to anything beyond mediocrity. I play for the love of the game, not out of any expectations of a single-digit handicap.

But, growing up, sport was a great ride while it lasted. Looking back, I did come away with more than the average person can imagine. In addition to a plethora of great memories and life-long friends, I feel that I came away from football – and sports in general – with more than I could ever repay. This holds true certainly for life and – and I was as surprised as anyone – for business as well. And it's these business lessons that I learned from football that are the subject of this book.

So, as one of my former coaches used to say, "Let's tee it up and kick it off."

Overview

Conventional wisdom has long praised the benefits of playing football in the development of the individual. Hard work. Teamwork. Discipline. Character building. Developing a never-say-die attitude. It's a fairly standard list. Legendary football coach Vince Lombardi said, "Football is a great deal like life in that it teaches that work, sacrifice, perseverance, competitive drive, selflessness and respect for authority is the price that each and every one of us must pay to achieve any goal that is worthwhile."

What's more, most of the same can be applied across the board to most any kind of athletic endeavor – especially the team sports. Basketball and baseball I know for sure. I never played hockey, but those who have have told me that it's all there as well.

This is not to say that the individual sports don't trigger their own inner qualities. They certainly do, and it even may be more intense, more focused. Tennis. Golf. Wrestling. Track – especially cross country. The commonalities are there. Hard work and discipline for starters. In the individual sports, those too require the individual to dig a little deeper, to call upon their own reserves, their own inner drives to achieve success.

There is a huge difference, however, between the team and individual sports. In the team sports, you win and lose as a team – as a group. When things are going badly, it's easy to hide. No such luxury, however, in the individual sports. There, you work alone. You train alone. You win and lose alone. You're out there – on center stage – for the world to see. Good or bad. And *that* is not easy.

I have long believed that there are – in general – as many lessons learned during college outside the classroom as in. Life lessons. People lessons. This is especially true when you go away to college. There, for the first time in your life, you're really on your own.

It's also my belief that people tend look past the non-academic lessons one can learn in college. But they're there. My experience with football bears this out.

I was an offensive end – tight end mostly although I did play some split end. As a tight end I was part-time interior offensive lineman and part-time receiver. This results in many different and many varied assignments. There was much to learn.

But there's more – beyond the conventional lists of lessons learned outside the classroom in college as well as those obvious lessons learned from athletics. There are lessons that I learned in football that can be applied specifically to the business world. As Coach Lombardi said, "Unless a man believes in himself and makes a total commitment to his career and puts everything he has into it – his mind, his body and his heart – what is life worth to him? If I were a salesman, I would make this commitment to my company, to the product and most of all, to myself."

Life lessons are wherever one can find them. Some are obvious; others less so. Over the years I have identified six situations in particular where I observed something through football and I was later able to see the relevance and application to the business world as well as my own career. The first two I learned from my older brother while in high school; three from my college coach; and the final lesson is more of a general, wide-ranging learning experience, but no less important.

In the postscript and epilogue, I'll point out a few more. But these six are the cornerstones – the ones that had the biggest impacts.

Lesson 1:

One Good Turn

In high school we had student equipment managers who were responsible for passing out and collecting equipment as well as handling peripheral items such as towels, tape, soap, etc. After a short time, it became apparent – even to the casual observer – that many of the players treated these *fellow students* like lower class citizens, servants – barking orders, wildly throwing equipment their way and so forth.

In college, the student equipment managers may have been part of the college work-study program and, as such, would have been paid. I don't know for certain, but that's not unlikely. In high school, however, the student equipment managers were not paid. Not ones to demonstrate any athletic prowess, they weren't about to be players. They did it to be part of the team – part of that intangible, extended family. The only genuine reward or recognition that they received was a varsity letter.

At the time, my brother (who preceded me in school by two years) pointed out that if you treated these managers well, lo and behold, they would return the favor in kind – and then some. Yes, shouting, "Hey manager. Gimme a towel!" would get you a towel. That fellow student typically would respond in his own space and time. Yes, you'll get your towel eventually – but nothing more.

Treating those volunteer workers with respect, however, would never fail to yield pretty much whatever you needed. Whether it was a clean, dry towel… or other useful perquisites such as a roll of tape that didn't exist for others. Maybe it was a piece of equipment that needed repair. A polite request and a heartfelt "thank you" paid dividends several times over. *Treat your support people as you would want to be treated.* A simple lesson, but an important one. It's a lesson that all successful businesses have accepted and put into practice on a daily basis.

In the book *In Search of Excellence,* authors Tom Peters and Robert Waterman Jr. state, "The good news comes from treating people decently and asking them to shine."

Hall of Fame basketball coach, UCLA's John Wooden said, "Friendship is two-sided. It isn't a friend just because someone's doing something nice for you. That's a nice person. There's friendship when you do for each other. It's like marriage – it's two-sided."

Unfortunately, this is concept that is not well known in the locker room. Actually there are many in business (albeit not enough) who have firmly grasped the concept. Noted publisher and humorist Bennett Cerf once stated, "A pat on the back, through only a few vertebrae removed from a kick in the pants, is miles ahead in results." Truer words were never spoken.

Is it surprising then, that business managers who treat their employees with respect and dignity have fewer labor problems, higher productivity, less strife, less turnover and longer tenure? Well-run companies (and they are out there) invariably treat their employees well. Not just financially, but with respect and dignity in their day-to-day dealings. And those companies are rewarded for it with employees who rarely leave, or who don't jump ship when someone dangles an insignificant pay raise in front of them. These are the employees who remain on the job beyond *quitting time,* staying for whatever additional time is required to ensure that the job is done and done correctly or that the customer is being satisfied. They don't necessarily do it for praise or more money, they do it because it's the right thing to do.

Companies (and managers) who treat their people well have employees who take pride in what they do and never (OK. Maybe rarely.) dread coming to work. All resulting in a happier work environment and subsequently a more profitable enterprise.

Ask any human resource manager about the benefits of low turnover and employee retention, and you will most likely get a lecture on the high costs associated with finding and hiring the right candidate, training that individual and how long it takes to return to full productivity. Some studies have shown that the cost of replacing an employee can be as high as 50–75 percent of that person's annual salary. For top management, it's even more – as much as 200 percent.

In other words, employee retention has a major impact on the bottom line.

This isn't rocket science. People want to be treated with respect regardless of the circumstances. As Lisa Quast recently wrote on forbes.com, "Respect isn't just something subordinates are forced to give managers. It's a valuable asset for employers to show and earn in the workplace. Earning employee respect isn't always easy, but when employers find ways to build respect at work, positive benefits ensue."

The amazing part of it is that it seems so simple, so obvious. Yet, it's so elusive. Why would you treat your employees any other way? They're working for you. They're devoting a significant portion of their lives to your endeavors. Think of the old adage, "You can catch more flies with honey." Between the carrot and the stick – which is universally more effective?

Management guru Peter Drucker once said, "Rank does not confer privilege or give power. It imposes responsibility."

Employers and management have a responsibility to their employees. Belittling them and taking them for granted creates an environment that no one wants to be part of. And that's why they leave, or maybe that's why no amount of money in raises or benefits ever quite seems to be enough. Does anyone really believe that treating people badly pays any dividends? Does being the autocratic boss really endear your employees to you? Will that make them want to come to work? Will any of your employees race to get to work on time just to be belittled by their boss? Or, at the other end of the day, will they be gone at 5:01 p.m. leaving projects undone? Or, will they leap at the first opportunity to jump ship and take a different job that pays marginally more or even the same amount?

Do you need to be Einstein to solve that equation?

LESSON #1

What worked in the high school locker room, works just as well in the workplace. Treat people with respect and dignity, and they will respond in kind. They will remain with your organization and provide years of service. And that loyalty can be found at the bottom line through lower costs for searching, hiring and retaining your people.

Lesson 2:

Know Your Stuff

On another other occasion, my brother shared with me a pearl of wisdom that I never forgot. He said, "If the coach knows that you know your assignments, he'll never be afraid to put you in the game."

On its surface, this doesn't come across as being profound. But it is.

Although our systems were not as complex as the modern game, we did have our playbooks with individual assignments and responsibilities. It was true then, just as it is now – not knowing what to do could cost a team dearly and earn you a stern reprimand from your coach. It didn't matter how good of an athlete you were, if you're in the wrong place or doing the wrong thing, that's a breakdown that dooms whatever play you're trying to run. Something, somewhere is not going to work. If you block the wrong opponent, who is going to block the player who is your responsibility?

Fans today complain a lot about "play calling." In football, with a few notable exceptions, it's not the play that's called, what matters is how well the play is executed. You can call the most creative, the most inventive play in the history of football – and you can call it at precisely the most opportune moment in the game – but if someone blocks the wrong defender – especially at the point of attack – it's all for naught. More on that later.

It doesn't even matter if you execute a perfect block, if it's the wrong player who you're blocking that means that your assigned player is free to move about untouched. That doesn't bode well for anyone and ultimately manifests itself on the scoreboard.

Know What You Need to Know

One day at practice in college, the second team was reviewing a play. The head coach asked the back-up tight end what his "rule" was on that play. [Unlike many other teams, we didn't have specific person blocking assignments as such. Rather we determined our assignments by blocking "rules." It was pretty ingenious. If you knew the rule on the play, it would apply to any defense. No matter what the defense threw at you, if you knew your rule, you were always aware of your correct assignment.]

Back to the story. When asked about his rule, the back-up tight end pointed at a defender and said, "I block him." (For the record, for that play, against that defense, he was correct.) The coach, however, responded with, "I didn't ask you who you block. I want to know what your rule is!" When the player finally admitted that he didn't know the rule, the coach yelled back to me, "Tab, what's your rule on this play?" I immediately responded, "Number 2 unless 3 is over or inside." (Don't ask. It would take too long to explain. But that was the rule.) "That's right," the coach yelled back. "Learn your rules."

That back-up actually may have been a better player, a better athlete than I was. But one reason that I was the starter was because the coach knew that I knew my assignments. I wouldn't cause a breakdown by doing the wrong thing, making a mental mistake.

Preparation Pays... and Pays

There is a story about the 1972 undefeated Miami Dolphins. The Dolphins middle linebacker Nick Buoniconti has been quoted as saying that "during the perfect season, the entire defense made seven mental mistakes all year."

Seven mental mistakes all year?! Seven?!

O.K. Let's do the math. There are 11 players on the field for each play – each with his own assignment. Various sources estimate that, on average, an NFL team will run approximately 65 plays per game. Eleven players at 65 plays per game, that's 715 player assignments per game. The '72 Dolphins played and won 17 games. Do the multiplication. At 715 assignments per game, those 17 games produced 12,155 player assignments for the entire season... and they had seven missed assignments. Seven! Out of 12,155 chances! That's a grade of 99.95 percent correct.

Looking at that, is it any wonder they were undefeated? The '72 Dolphins defense was, what the media dubbed, "the no-name defense" because they didn't have any marquee players. However, when you're not making mistakes, do you really need high profile players? The sage of the New York Yankees, Yogi Berra, once observed, "Some things are just too coincidental to be a coincidence."

There is a school of thought that says that games aren't won as much as they're lost. And they're lost by the team that makes the most mistakes. Long-time Cleveland Browns' Hall of Fame coach Paul Brown once said, "Football is a game of errors. The team that makes the fewest errors in a game usually wins."

Is that any different in business? You've got to make a presentation to management, or to a large potential customer. When you're successful, how many times do you practice your presentation? How carefully and thoroughly do you research and study your subject matter? How closely do you monitor the competition? How well do you anticipate questions and objections? How many businesses have failed because they underestimated the competition or they failed to accurately gauge changes in the marketplace? The simple answer is: a lot.

Being confident in your knowledge of your material, takes a lot of the pressure off of what could be a stressful situation. Legendary Pittsburgh Steeler coach Chuck Noll observed, "Pressure is something you feel when you don't know what you're doing."

When you've done it right, when you know your subject inside and out, aren't you more comfortable *and* more confident? And don't think for one second that your confidence won't come across to your audience. They will know. And it will invariably affect the outcome in a positive manner.

When you've done your homework, when you've learned your assignments, good things generally happen. Iconic college basketball coach Bobby Knight said, "The will to succeed is important, but the what's more important is the will to prepare."

My college roommate and teammate worked in the paint business for decades. People in the paint business like to talk about how well the paint goes on, how it looks, how well it covers, how many mils thick the paint is, how well it endures the elements, how long it lasts, etc. That's all true, but according to my friend, the company preached that the most important part of a paint job is *surface preparation*. If your surface is well prepared, the paint is that much more likely to work the way it's intended. Period.

Whether it's learning who to block on the power sweep or 18-ISO, or learning about your customer base or your competitors – the resulting advantage is no accident. What's more, the coach – er, boss – is sure to recognize and reward those who are prepared and treat those who are not accordingly.

It has nothing to do with luck. My high school coach was always quick to point out that *"luck* is what happens when preparation meets opportunity." Former Arkansas, Notre Dame and South Carolina football coach Lou Holtz has noted, "The man who complains about the way the ball bounces is likely to be the one who dropped it."

Knowing your assignments and preparing for them, it goes a long way in football, in business and in life. Preparation pays even when you're not actually playing or preparing for the game. Getting in shape for the season is a form of preparation that can pay special dividends.

Preparing for the Season

Earlier, I mentioned the Early Morning Track Club. To avoid membership, you had to make your assigned time in running a mile. In my sophomore year, my time was five minutes and 45 seconds (5:45). (For some reason, junior year it was an even six minutes and senior year it went back to 5:45. It was a coaching decision. No explanation needed.)

While working out during the summer before sophomore year, I realized that I could run a 90-second quarter mile with a minimum amount of effort as well as minimum wear and tear. I reasoned that if I maintained that pace over four quarter miles, my time in the mile would be six minutes. Suddenly I thought, "At that pace, all I have to do is cut 15 seconds off my total time, and I'm home free without really killing myself!"

So how to do that? We ran our miles in the stadium around the football field where each lap was one-quarter mile. Four laps and you've got your mile.

I thought that if I could run the first quarter mile (lap) just keeping up with whomever was setting the pace, that would probably shave a few seconds (maybe 5-10?) off my total time. Good strategy, I thought.

With that, I could downshift into my cruise mode and cover the middle two laps in 90 seconds each without overly burdening myself. However, for the final lap, I would still need to cut another 5-10 seconds.

Don't ask why, because I don't know, but when I would run my mile during my own summer workouts, at no one's suggestion or recommendation, I would "kick" around the last turn of the last lap – the final 110 yards. I would hesitate to call it a sprint, but when I made that final turn, I gave it everything I had left through to the finish line.

So my strategy was: keep up with the first-lap pacesetter, conserve my energy during the middle two laps, and use my ending kick in the final lap. Mix in a little adrenalin and I figured I was good to go.

So the time came to run my mile. The first thing I noticed was that we were starting (and would ultimately end) at about the 30-yard line – unlike the 50-yard line start/finish I used during my workouts. I reasoned that this would be good for me for it would give me an additional 20 yards of sprint at the end. I knew it could only help.

Unfortunately, during the first lap, I realized that there was a fly in the ointment. I was in a group of about six players. We started running and by the time we rounded the first curve, I looked for the guy who was setting the pace. Oops! It was me.

So the first-lap pacesetter turned out to be me and my own adrenalin. It worked well enough and I finished the first lap in about 80 seconds. After the first lap I slowed down to my 90-second per lap pace for the middle two laps.

I thought my plan was working. The coaches didn't. One coach in particular began to chastise me for slowing down, thinking that I was quitting, that I was running out of gas. He didn't know my plan.

Fortunately, the last lap went accordingly to my script. When I reached the final curve, I began to give it everything I had. I made it through to the finish line, logging a time of five minutes, 40 seconds (5:40) – five seconds ahead of my time. I was totally drained, but totally relieved.

Preparation Breeds Trust

There's another aspect of being prepared that applies equally to football as well as business. When the coaches (bosses) recognize that you're prepared, that you know your assignments (the product, the company, the competition, etc.), they're more willing to trust you and to give you additional responsibilities – and (many times) ultimately more money.

When running our offense senior year in college, in addition to our set formations, we also had variations off them for special situations or to gain some special advantage. One of these we called a "tailor." Normally the tight end lines up right next to the offensive tackle. But with a tailor adjustment, the tight end moves out about three yards. You're not really a split end, but you're not tight with the rest of the offensive line either.

Many times when we would tailor the tight end, it would cause the defense to make some sort of adjustment and the coaches were always eager to know what adjustments the defense would make. Because they trusted my judgment, especially early in the game I had the freedom to tailor on plays where my alignment wouldn't make a difference – to us. However, when I lined up in a tailor, the coaches in the press box could see how the defense would react and, if it was to our advantage, call certain plays with the tight end tailored.

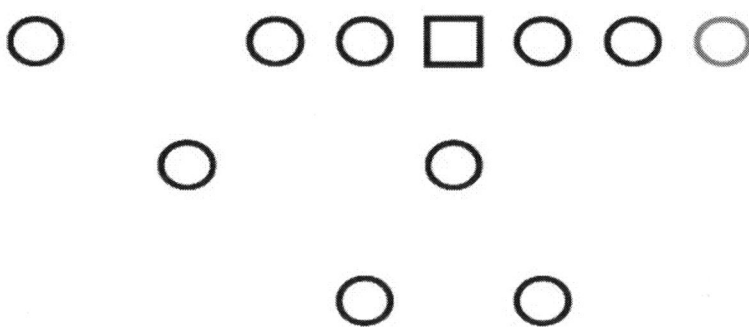

**Standard formation
with a split left end, tight right end**

Normally, when a tailor was called, I would move directly to my spot – three yards split from the offensive tackle. To alert the coaches in the press box, when I would run a "dummy tailor" – one that I did on my own, I would initially stand next to the offensive tackle, but before getting down in my stance, I would move out three yards to the tailored position. That would signal the coaches in the press box that this was a dummy tailor.

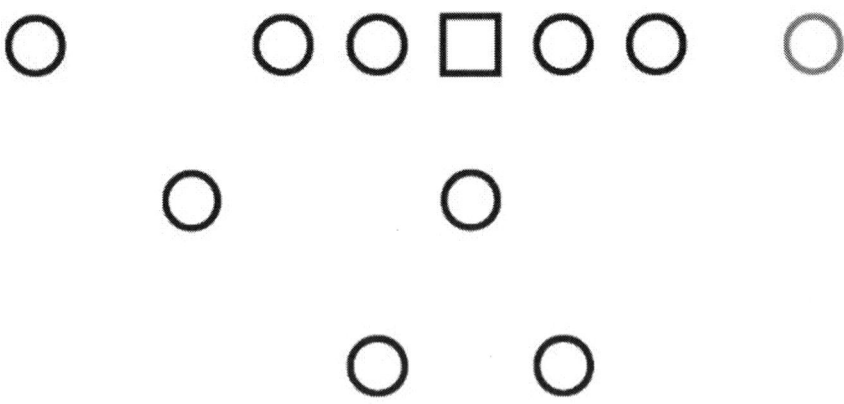

Standard formation with the split end left and the tight end "tailored"

The point is that because they trusted my knowledge of the play and of me knowing my assignments, they allowed me this extra freedom, or responsibility. The same holds true in business. When bosses are confident in your knowledge and your preparation, they are much more willing to give you additional freedom, leeway, responsibility and remuneration.

So, the bottom line for business: What's the lesson? Do your homework. Know what you need to know to achieve whatever your goal is. UCLA's Coach Wooden observed, "Things turn out best for the people who make the best of the way things turn out."

LESSON #2

Do your homework. Know what you need to do to achieve whatever your goal is. Develop a strategy. Create a plan. Execute that plan. Carry the day.

Lesson 3:

Marching Orders

How many times do you hear about employees who complain about being left in the dark about what the company is doing, why the boss is doing what he's doing, why are we doing such and such in this manner? It's not an uncommon plight. How much simpler is it when everyone knows what direction they're headed and what the destination is; what the overall aim or objective is.

I had a client that made additives for plastics. Their products ended up being used in some pretty high profile applications, but the employees didn't know that. In fact, the employees had little idea how their products were used at all.

I suggested that they obtain some large photographs of some their more noteworthy installations, frame and matte them, and display them around the company with explanations of how their company's products were being used. The employees loved it! They began bragging about where their work was being used. Because they understood, they took more pride and put more enthusiasm in their work. They now valued what they, and the company, were doing.

Setting the Tone

When I arrived in college, Edinboro football had a dismal history. In 44 years of competition prior to my senior year, they had experienced only five winning seasons. Not five championships (there were no championships), but five years where they won more than they lost – five out of 44! We were the doormats of the conference. Whenever possible, opponents scheduled Edinboro for their homecoming games – because they knew that, against us, they had a good chance of winning.

In the fall of my sophomore year, we won two and lost seven. One week following our final game, the head coach was dismissed. He won only five games in three years.

A new coach was hired in January of my sophomore year. A few weeks later, we had our first team meeting with him. The players were dutifully assembled in one of the big lecture halls. We were there, but where was the coach?

After a couple of minutes, in he strode. Without a word or a nod, he walked directly to the front of the room where there was one of those two-sided chalk boards. He picked up a piece of chalk and wrote on the board:

C-H-A-M-P-I-O-N-S-H-I-P-!

He turned around, looked at us and said, "Gentlemen, that's why I'm here."

I turned to my roommate who was sitting next to me and said, "I think I'm gonna like this guy."

From that point forward, there was no doubt that he planned to whip us into shape, not only to win more games, not only to win more than we lost, but the ultimate goal was to win a championship. That was the objective. That's what his vision was for us. That was the direction that we were going.

[For the record, in his first season we won as many as we lost. In my senior year, his second season, we won that championship – the first football championship in Edinboro history. Even today, after decades of success, that 1970 season is still held up as the "gold standard" – as one coach called it – for Edinboro football teams to strive for.]

Vince Lombardi said, "Individual commitment to a group effort – that is what makes a team work, a company work, a society work, a civilization work."

Our coach was the boss. There was no doubt in anyone's mind about that. He determined the end result of the "group effort." He set the goal. He established the vision. There was no doubt in anyone's mind as to what his expectations were. From that moment on, every player on the team, every player in the program, everyone who was in any way, shape or form connected with that football program knew what the goal was; what we were working toward; where he ultimately expected us to go.

Coach Lombardi also said, "Success demands singleness of purpose." We had that.

What's Your Mission?
What's Your Vision?

So too in business. Companies spend countless hours developing their mission and vision statements. Most are psychobabble-like drivel. The good ones are not. Good or bad how many mission and vision statements end up in someone's desk drawer or tucked neatly in a file cabinet. Nowadays it's simple to put your mission and vision statements on the company website. Yet, how often are they referred to, called attention to. How many companies actually heed to their missions? How few employees even know what they are, and fewer still have ever read them or know what they contain?

The most successful companies have iconic mission statements that are short and to the point. "At American Express we have a mission to be the world's most respected service brand." Simple. "Nordstrom works relentlessly to give customers the most compelling shopping experience possible." Direct.

Many companies have used advertising campaigns to crystalize their missions and visions. Not only are they memorable, they speak succinctly to what the company and/or product does or represents. FedEx: "Absolutely, positively has to be there overnight." BMW: "Ultimate Driving Machine."

What's more, the really successful ones last for decades. DeBeers' "A Diamond is Forever" dates back to 1948. Wheaties: "Breakfast of Champions," can trace its roots back to the late 1920s.

Whether it's Edinboro football under Bill McDonald, or working for American Express, Nordstrom or BMW, when you know what the vision is, you know where you're headed, you're that much more likely to get there.

LESSON #3
When everyone knows where they're going, it's easy to lead and easier to get on board and easier still to ensure the trip's success.

Lesson 4:

No Man is an Island

One day at practice in college, I noticed that our head coach was simply wandering around the practice field. The team had been broken up into small groups by position. Occasionally the coach would stop to watch the offensive line, then the defensive backs, then linebackers, then the defensive line and the offensive backs.

I remember watching him and thinking, "He's the head coach, but he's not *doing* anything!" It wasn't until later that I realized that he had already done his work... and that involved hiring competent, knowledgeable assistant coaches to work with his players. Together they planned what was to be covered in practice and how that would be applied at game time. In short, he had delegated some of his coaching authority to them.

Isn't this also true in business? Absolutely. According to Wikipedia, delegation is "one of the core concepts of management leadership."

Some of the most successful business entities are quick to chime in as well. The Harvard School of Business, the Wharton School, Forbes, Fortune, etc., etc. They all preach the benefits and wisdom of delegation. Lee Iaccoca. Jack Welch. Warren Buffet. Steve Jobs. Bill Gates. They're all on board.

Do you want the textbook definition? Management consultant Carol Hacker notes, "Delegation is a complex management skill that few people master without guidance. And that's the sticking point. Most managers are never really taught how to delegate the right way. They were promoted to a leadership role and just told to delegate and get results through other people. As a result, delegation doesn't happen as often or as smoothly as it should."

So what does make it work? The simple answer is: a lot.

Start with having a clear idea of what and what not to delegate. This is part of establishing trust with your subordinates and not allowing them to feel that you're simply pushing off onto them things that you just don't want to do. Also – and for some people, this can be the most difficult part – don't be afraid to let it go. Let them do the job you're asking them to do. It helps if you make certain that you use your communications skills so they know precisely what is expected of them and that you select the right person for each assignment.

When Edward J. DeBartolo Jr. owned the San Francisco 49ers, they won five Super Bowls. During a recent radio interview, he explained his take on successful NFL ownership. In as many words he said, find and hire competent football people, then get out of their way and allow them to do the job you hired them to do.

And don't be afraid that they will fail. Some inevitably will. Most will not. Or, maybe they won't do things the way that you would have done it. Get over it. Get over yourself. It's not about being right. It's not about doing it right. It's about getting it done.

I was in a meeting with a colleague and a client. The client mentioned some task that needed to be completed. Immediately, my colleague responded, "We can make that happen."

On our way out to the parking lot I said to him, "We can't do that!"

He replied, "I know. I didn't say that we were going to do it. I said, 'We can make that happen.' We'll find somebody to do it." And we did. And the client was happy. And our subcontractor was happy. And we made money. End of story.

The *Harvard Business Review* states that delegation requires redefining competence as "helping others to do great work," instead of "doing great work all by myself."

Is business really that different from football?

The more I thought about it, the more I realized that a successful head coach does little actual coaching. These is especially true in today's top college programs as well as the pro ranks. The head coach spends a significant amount of his time as the boss, the administrator, the CEO, the face of the team in dealing with the media. He has other people handle the day-in, day-out football particulars for him. His job is to ensure that it all gets done and gets done correctly.

Getting Done the Ho-Hum

This was also true off the field – even for something as mundane as planning an away game. Once I happened to notice an assignment sheet the head coach prepared for a road trip. Each assistant coach had his job(s) to do. One assistant to pass out and collect hotel keys. Another made sure all the players were present and accounted for on the team bus. Another was responsible for the pre-game meal, etc. Again, he had delegated responsibility – not unlike the successful manager or entrepreneur conducting everyday business.

Once again, the successful coaches know this. "Whatever you do in life, surround yourself with smart people who'll argue with you." – John Wooden

Without the burden of the minutia, our coach was able to focus on the big picture – as all successful managers do.

LESSON #4

Don't try to do it all yourself. Surround yourself with good people and give them the freedom to do what they do best. Then get out of their way and let them have at it.

Lesson 5:

Quality Throughout

Finally, when my playing days ended, my college coach conducted "exit interviews" with all the departing seniors – which is, in and of itself, a laudable business practice. But that's another story.

As the conclusion of my senior season approached, I became very concerned about walking away from football "cold turkey" as it was. Football – and other sports – had been a major part of my life for more than a decade and now, all at once, it was going to end. Over. Gone. Never to return.

I wondered if I could sort of hang around and ease my way out of it. Because I wouldn't be graduating until the following December, I thought I could help as a graduate assistant during spring practice and, in the following fall, work with the freshman team as well. As it turned out, I did both and additionally traveled with one of the assistant coaches and did some scouting for the varsity as well. Talk about a lesson in preparation! But, again, that's another story.

Back to my interview. When I mentioned my desire to *hang around* to the coach, he responded that he was glad because he felt that I was a quality person, and "We want quality people associated with our program," he said.

We continued to discuss that concept and he summed up the importance of quality people with: "You know, you can win games with good athletes, but to win championships, you need good people." He then added with a sly, little grin – as he had written on the chalkboard nearly two years earlier, "And we're all about winning championships."

And he wasn't alone. According to Hall of Fame coach Don Shula, "The one thing that I know is that you win with good people."

Although both of these comments were football specific, the same concept can be just as easily applied to any business, any company, any endeavor. Business advice from any number of sources contains admonitions such as "hire good people"; "surround yourself with good people"; etc.

Good People Make Good Business

Today, businesses immerse themselves with TQM, Six-Sigma, ISO 9000, ISO 14000 and so forth. These are all worthy pursuits but they are mostly focused on products and processes. Whether its manufacturing on the shop floor or bolstering the sales staff, the human element must never be overlooked. Basketball's John Wooden recognized this, "I worry that business leaders are more interested in material gain than they are in having the patience to build up a strong organization, and a strong organization starts with caring for their people."

But it goes beyond caring for people. Like the saying goes, you have to surround yourself with good people: People who buy into your proposition. People who are dedicated to the cause. People who are committed to going the extra mile when necessary.

How often do you hear about players today having substance abuse issues and brushes with the law. Are those the kind of people you want on your team? Iconic Alabama football coach Paul "Bear" Bryant said, "I make my practices real hard because if a player is a quitter, I want him to quit in practice, not in a game." That's one way to separate the wheat from the chaff.

To no one's great surprise, good people do good things. Just as it was with the '72 Miami Dolphins. When you start with good people, teach them well; prepare them well; and let them execute their jobs, good things tend to happen. It's no accident.

Good People Do Good Things

A recent example of this is the 2015 Super Bowl when, late in the game, the Seattle Seahawks were within striking distance of scoring a touchdown and winning the game. Instead, they had a pass attempt intercepted at the goal line which secured victory for the New England Patriots. Seattle coach Pete Carroll was widely criticized for his play call.

The conventional wisdom said that he should have given the ball to his running back Marshawn Lynch. "If you have one of the best running backs in the game today, why would you pass?" one commentator said.

Well, let's review. Go back and watch that play again – it's on YouTube. If you look at the teams before the ball is snapped, it's fairly obvious that there were *at least* two New England defenders keying directly on Lynch. On the previous play, Lynch was stuffed when they tried to run him into the end zone. On the play in question Lynch was used as a decoy. It's a technique or strategy often used in football. Unfortunately for the Seahawks, when the ball was snapped,

Lynch's attempt at being a decoy consisted of merely making a half-hearted run to the left. He never even feigned to look back for the ball minimizing his effectiveness as a decoy.

There are any number of offensive theorists who reason that the best way to beat a defense is to do what they're not expecting. Take what the defense is giving you. Chuck Noll won four Super Bowls with Pittsburgh and he once noted that every defense has a weak spot and it's up to the offense to determine what that weak spot is and exploit it.

It was reasonable that New England would be waiting on Lynch and throw everything they had at him.

So, if the defense was expecting Lynch to get the ball and wasn't expecting the pass play – in the opposite direction, no less – why did it fail? Three reasons.

First, after taking the snap, Seattle quarterback Russell Wilson looked at only one thing. He never looked anywhere else. He was totally locked in on Ricardo Lockette, the primary receiver. The intended receiver would have been obvious to anyone in the New England secondary who was paying attention.

Two, Lockette still was wide open – for at least a healthy second – more than enough time for an experienced, competent NFL quarterback to get the ball to him. But Wilson hesitated and didn't deliver the ball until the defense had the chance to react and close in.

Third, Wilson laid the ball out in front of the receiver where the receiver *and* the defender had an equal chance at catching it. An experienced NFL quarterback would have thrown the pass slightly behind the receiver. If the ball had been thrown slightly behind the receiver – so that the receiver would have had to turn slightly to his left to catch it, the defender would have to have *gone through* the receiver to get it. Unless the officials are sleeping, that's still a penalty.

The bottom line is: Seattle failed. But it wasn't because of the play that was called. That play failed because of the manner in which it was executed. And, make no mistake, Malcom Butler, the New England defender, made an outstanding play when he intercepted the pass. But, with a lackluster decoy, by not looking anywhere else, by hesitating in delivering the ball, and by not throwing an accurate pass, the Seahawks played right into his hands.

When you know your assignments – *and execute them* – good things happen.

Jimmy Johnson, winner of back-to-back Super Bowls with the Dallas Cowboys once said, "It's not how many great plays you make; it's how few bad ones you make. I know fans, and even some losing coaches, are enamored with long pass completions or the great run plays, but that doesn't offset the interception or the fumble."

Something for Seattle fans to consider.

Similar to my earlier point, it all comes down to people. As for play calling, it's not the play, it's the people running the play. Just like, it's not the golf club; it's the guy holding the club. In baseball, it's not the bat, it's the guy holding the bat.

"First and Foremost, We're a People Business"

Over the years, the need for "good people" has never diminished – especially in competitive times like these. Companies that simply want to get *bodies* through the door, pay for it in the long run.

I worked for a company that had hundreds of sales representatives all over the country. The company sold about 13,000 different items into the automotive and industrial aftermarkets. There wasn't much fancy or sophisticated about the vast majority of these products. Most were everyday commodities that a lot of businesses needed.

When a sales rep would leave the company, the district manager was under a lot of pressure to fill that spot as soon as possible. They were instructed to keep someone in the field calling on the customers in that area so that the competition wouldn't swoop in and take that business. While that's all well and good, many managers felt the need to just get "a body" in there quickly with or without support and little (if any) training. That tends to create what some wieners might call "a sticky situation."

Without any backup, with minimal support, not surprisingly, there were territories that turned over three and even four times per year. Many of those hires probably never should have been hired in the first place. They just were not the right people for the post – and it showed.

In the end, everyone paid. The company lost sales. The managers made more work for themselves by hiring for the same job three or four times per year. The sales reps – especially the ones who left quickly – suffered as well. Oh, yes. And let's not forget the customers. They suffered too. Especially the ones who didn't abandon the company for a competitor.

Those managers who took the time to find a suitable representative – one who was dedicated, responsible and a quick study – saw their turnover rate among the lowest in the company. Their sales teams were more stable, more productive and more successful. What a surprise!

Regardless of the business or industry, those companies that take their time to ensure that every employee is an outstanding individual will find their workforce is one that is highly motivated, easily trainable, exceptionally productive, always cooperative and forever willing to "go the extra yard" to ensure the company's success.

Years after my college playing days were done, I was speaking with one of our assistant coaches who told me, "You know, I coached for 35 years and that team (the championship team from my senior year) was the most *coachable* team I ever saw. We would tell you guys to do something, and you did it!"

And it showed.

LESSON #5

Granted, winning individual games is a good thing. But, in the final analysis – in athletics or in business – isn't the goal to win the championship? To be the best? To be on top? Good people will help you do just that.

Lesson Six:

Back to Basics

One characteristic shared by contemporary football and present-day business, is that they both have raised the complexity of what they do to previously unimagined heights.

In football you've got a myriad of concepts, fads and trends — the west coast offense, run 'n gun, the wildcat, the nickel defense, the 46 defense, the constant shuttling of players in and out the game to secure favorable matchups and more. Even when I played, we ran a "triple option" where, at the snap of the ball, we had no idea who would be the ultimate ball carrier. It could have been the fullback, the tailback, or the quarterback. It was all dependent on how the quarterback read the defense and how it reacted after the ball was snapped.

Of late, even the size of a quarterback's hands has suddenly become a topic of intense scrutiny. Really? Does anyone really believe that a quarterback's hands are more important than his brains, his heart and his gut.

The Wall Street Journal reported on an analysis that was done on NFL quarterbacks, comparing their performances while taking the center snap while in the shotgun formation as opposed to taking the snap under center. Some statistical analysis firm actually went back ten years, reviewing every snap from every game. For the record, they found that when quarterbacks take the snap from center, their quarterback ratings are roughly 20 percent higher than when they line up in the shotgun. Yet the vast majority of pro plays today begin in the shotgun. Go figure.

The Business of Big Data

Take a glance at baseball for a moment. There is a sport virtually drowning in statistics. Today we know if a left-handed batter hits better against right-handed pitchers in day games as opposed to night. We know hitters' batting averages when they're behind or ahead in the count. Consider the number crunching and analysis that was portrayed in the movie "Moneyball" as practiced in real life by the Oakland A's. In that movie, the A's probably were the first to implement the business concept of "Big Data."

Speaking of Big Data, in a *Wall Street Journal* report, consulting firm McKinsey & Company noted that today companies have incredible mountains of data at their fingertips. Production data. Delivery data. Sales data. Customer data. They know who is likely to buy something, at what time of day they're likely to buy it, the manner in which they buy it, etc. McKinsey noted that companies are drowning in the amount of data that they have amassed and are continuing to amass.

The problem, they note, is that while most companies are swimming in a sea of data, most have no one who can purposefully and accurately analyze that data. They have all this information at the ready but they don't know what to do with it or worse, they don't know what it's telling them.

The author (far left) huddles
at practice with his teammates.

It's a Learning Situation

When things get out of hand in education, the rallying cry often seems to be that we need to go *back to basics*. There's a cerebral breakthrough.

In education the basics are reading, writing and arithmetic. In football, the basics are blocking and tackling.

In business, the basics also are not that complicated. In the book *Business – An Integrative Approach,* business basics are defined as "providing goods and services that meet customer needs." Sounds simple enough.

In Search of Excellence focuses its basic attention squarely on the customer, "Customers reign supreme. They are not treated to untested technology or unnecessary goldplating. They are the recipients of products that last, service delivered promptly."

As with so many other things, if it was easy, everyone would do it. But alas, they don't. Many studies point out that approximately 80 percent of start-up companies fail roughly within their first two years. In nature, it's only the strong who survive. Maybe in business, it should be only the smart survive. Merely surviving in the hyper-competitive world of global business is an accomplishment in itself.

The Test of Time

A bellwether of business performance is the Dow Jones Average (formerly the Dow Jones Industrial Average.) For decades analysts have claimed that the companies on "the Dow" signify the best of their class. How they perform is supposed to be representative of how the entire economy is performing. According to Wikipedia (and others), the Dow Jones Average was first compiled on May 26, 1896 and measured only 12 companies. Interestingly, of the original 12 industrials, only General Electric endures to this day. The rest have either gone out of business or have been bought and sold so many times that they bear little resemblance to the companies they once were.

Can football be reduced to a simple statement or concept? Earlier we stated that the basics of football were blocking and tackling. Legendary coach Vince Lombardi echoed that sentiment, "Some people try to find things in this game that don't exist but football is only two things - blocking and tackling."

Lombardi also added that if you block better than the other team and if you tackle better than the other team, you're likely going to beat the other team.

In business and football alike, the basics rule the day. If you consistently take care of your customer; if you regularly block and tackle better than your opponents, you'll win. You'll win on the football field, and you'll win in the field of business.

A little different

This lesson is somewhat different from the others noted in this book. Here, there are no specific anecdotes of practice or game experience from which to draw. There are no war stories. But there are best practices.

In high school, before every practice and before every game, we did STB – stance, tackling and blocking. The team paired off; everyone got in their stances and the coaches reviewed and critiqued as necessary. Then we blocked – aiming your nose at the other player's belt buckle, hitting that, gathering your feet underneath you and driving for a few yards. Finally, we tackled. You hit the opposing player in the mid-section, wrapped your arms around him, lifted and carried him a couple of yards.

No specific STB stands out because we did it religiously everyday. Every game. Every practice.

Maybe that's because "back to basics" is just that. It's so basic that, if it's not there everyday, every practice, every game, it can't be summoned on a moment's notice. If you haven't been blocking well all year, what makes you think that you'll be able to pull it off on that third and one when the game is on the line? If you haven't been mastering your tackling skills everyday, every practice, what makes you think that you can make that game-saving tackle?

There is a business story – or maybe it's just an urban legend. Who knows? But it worth re-telling because illustrates the point.

Supposedly, there was a pet food company that was introducing a new product – a new dog food. They hired a branding agency to name the product and to determine its market position. They hired a design firm to create eye-catching, alluring graphics for the packaging. They did market research to determine how to position the new product and at what price level it should be placed. They confirmed their distribution channels and developed a killer marketing introduction plan. They did everything right.

When the product launched it was an immediate success… for a while. The company quickly discovered that their strong initial sales were not carrying through. There was little repeat business. Within a year the product was pulled from the shelves and relegated to the scrap heap of product history.

But they did everything right. Well, almost.

In all their planning and research, in all their design work, despite all their distribution and marketing efforts, they failed. It seems that they were so busy doing all the right things, they overlooked one critical, business basic. They never tested it on dogs to see if the animals liked it and would eat it. Apparently, the canine vote didn't like it and wouldn't eat it. It didn't take long for the customer/dog owner/decision-maker to stop buying it and ultimately, for the company to stop selling it.

Doing the basics in sports extends to the fan base as well – which, on a professional level – is the business portion of the sport.

I had the opportunity to interview one of baseball's legendary owners and promoters, Bill Veeck. (Veeck is best known for planting the ivy at Wrigley Field; sending a midget up to bat in St. Louis; setting an attendance record and winning the World Series with the Cleveland Indians in 1948; implementing the first exploding scoreboard; and he was the first to put names on the backs of players uniforms.)

At the time of our interview, drawing a million fans in attendance was still the gold standard for major league baseball. With that in mind, Veeck imparted one of the best business lessons I ever heard. He said, "You've got to remember, when you draw a million people to the ballpark in a season, it's not a million different people. Anyone can get them to come once, the trick is to get them to come back."

LESSON #6

Benjamin Franklin advised, "If you take care of the pennies, the dollars will take care of themselves." So too, in football – blocking and tackling. So too, in business, make a good product, take good care of your customers. Adhering to simple, basic concepts typically produces the greatest amount of success.

The Post-Game Interview

Yes, participating in football does teach character, teamwork, discipline, etc. But there is more there to learn in the whole experience than readily meets the eye. Whether it's victories on the football field or success in the world of business – treating people well, knowing your assignments, delegating responsibility, setting and communicating your goals, the need for good people and the need to pay attention to the basics – these six simple lessons help separate the winners from the losers.

My college roommate and I have talked many times over the years about how fortunate we were during our playing days. We had great coaches. They weren't household names like Brown, Shula, Noll, Wooden or Lombardi. They were McDonald, Ruvolo, Watson, Hyland, Bowen, Straub, Gilstrap, Shesman and many more. And they knew football. They knew how to win. And they knew how to coach. They knew how to make football transcend being just a game. They made it a microcosm of life.

Many years later we had a reunion of the Edinboro team from my senior year. In addressing the group, Bill McDonald, our head coach noted, "You know, we had a pretty good year on the field in 1970, but we've done alright since then as well. Of all our players, 95 percent graduated. [An aside: the NCAA average at the time was about 55 percent.] The team produced three Ph.D.'s. Five guys own their own businesses. The team produced 26 coaches, 19 head coaches, three college head coaches and one of the high school head coaches won a *USA Today* national championship." Apparently, somebody did something right.

Not surprisingly, Vince Lombardi said it best, "I firmly believe that any man's finest hour, the greatest fulfillment of all that he holds dear, is the moment when he has worked his heart out in a good cause and lies exhausted on the field of battle victorious."

Post Scripts

Those six lessons are only the big picture examples that have stuck in my mind over time. There are more snippets that one might find helpful while navigating through the world of business and the business of life. Here are just three.

The New Assignment. Want to endear yourself to your boss? Volunteer and/or be willing to accept new assignments. Being willing to do so without whining and complaining will go along way to earning the boss's respect and will earn you a spot as being viewed as a valuable member of the team.

Through the first half of my junior year in college, I was the starting tight end. One Monday in the middle of the season, I went to the stadium for practice and happened to wander into the coaches' offices. The head coach was sitting behind a desk and called me over when I entered. "Oh, I'm glad you're here," he said. (Who's kidding who? It was Monday afternoon, where else would I be?) Then he continued – and note the language, "The coaches were talking… and we *think*… we *might*… want you to learn the split end position."

Without hesitation, I said, "OK. I don't have my playbook here. It's in my dorm room. But I'll take a look at it tonight and you tell me what you want me to do."

"Oh, great. Great. Glad to hear that," he replied.

Less than an hour later when we were at practice and he called for "that first offense," I went to my usual spot in the huddle where the tight end stood. The head coach turned around, looked at me and said, "Get over here," gesturing to the spot where the split end stood, "You're playing split end now."

"I guess they made their decision," I thought… making me possibly the only player in football history to be converted into a wide receiver – just to block. Yeah, we didn't throw the ball very much.

The postscript to this story is when the quarterback came into the huddle and called a play, I turned to the coach to ask, "OK. What do I do?" He then proceeded to lambaste me for not knowing my assignment. "Hey," I thought – I didn't dare say it out loud, "Remember me? Thirty seconds ago I was playing a different position." Even though I didn't have an opportunity to prepare (as noted earlier), not knowing an assignment didn't sit well with him – under any circumstances.

Looking back, that didn't matter to the coach. He was confident that I would learn the position in time for Saturday's game. In the final analysis, what did matter was that I was willing to take on a new assignment – willingly and without complaint. And by Saturday, I learned it and was up to speed on the assignments for the split end position and was able to execute my assignments as needed.

I was willing to do whatever he needed for the good of the team. Isn't the same true in business? You need someone to stay an hour late, come in an hour early, or work on a Saturday? Most good bosses know who to ask and why. And, most good bosses (and, yes, I know, the key word there is "good") recognize that. They also appreciate it and reward those who do it.

There is another line of thinking that says if you want to get something done, give it to a busy person. Be wary of giving it to someone who then sighs several weeks later that the assignment wasn't done because he was "too busy." Comedian Drew Carey once remarked that there's a support group for people who are busy, it's called "Everybody."

Repetition. Vince Lombardi once said, "Winning is a habit." How true. Is there any need to explain that connection to business? But sometimes it's the little things that matter and doing them correctly, repetitively shows.

As part of our pre-practice routine my senior year in college, the coaches had us do "form running." I know it sounds stupid, but there is some rationale behind it.

Form running consisted of running about 30 yards at half to three-quarter speed. The idea was that while you were running, rather than focusing on how fast you were going at the time, you concentrated on the individual physical aspects of running – pumping your arms, extending your legs, landing on and pushing off the balls of your feet, etc.

The coaches added that, when pumping your arms, the natural tendency is to form a fist. They explained that, when you form a fist, you tighten all the muscles in your arms and shoulders. They felt that the ideal, however, was to keep your arms and shoulders loose, almost relaxed. To accomplish this, they said that you should eschew the fist and run with your fore finger and thumb touching. That would tend to keep your arms relaxed.

I never gave it a second thought. I just did it everyday at practice because they said it would help and I didn't want to get yelled at for not doing it.

For the record, I never felt that I moved any faster. In fact, when looking at some game film years later, my initial reaction was, "I don't remember being that slow." Be that as it may, I followed their regimen of holding my thumb and fore finger together.

Here's the clincher. After the season ended, I was looking at some game photographs. In one picture, you could see me running down field looking for someone to block. On closer inspection, you can see my right hand where my forefinger and thumb were touching – just like form running in practice.

As you can see from the nearby photo, the daily repetitive practice of holding the thumb and forefinger together (see circle) carried over to game day.

Had anyone told me that I ran like that at the time, I would never have believed that I was doing it. But, as they say, pictures don't lie. In reviewing some other photos, I saw myself doing it on several other occasions. Apparently, the repetition made it stick – without me even realizing it.

Repetition. Do things enough times and they become habits. Even when you don't realize it. The same is true in football. The same is true in business. The same is true in life.

Focus. Are there any business gurus around who don't emphasize the importance of being focused? You focus on the bottom line, or the top line. You focus on new products. You focus on market or industry penetration. You focus on emerging markets. You focus on your customers. You focus on your competitors. Whatever your business, whatever your circumstances, there is a need – at some level – for focus.

The importance of focus can be granular as well. Focusing on a new manufacturing process or procedure. Focus on automating or computerizing one function or another. Focus on training or re-training your staff. You continuously are focused on something.

Of course, that's true on the football field as well. Focus on developing a new quarterback. Focus on improving the offensive or defensive lines. Focus on improving special teams. All these lists can go on and on.

My senior year in college we had a pre-season scrimmage against a nearby small college. Throughout the entire scrimmage, I was biding my time to have the opportunity to block one particular player. He typically lined up to my outside where I really didn't have the opportunity to take him on.

Near the end of the day, we were running goal-line offense – against their goal-line defense. In this situation the player in question lined up in the end-tackle gap just to my inside, making him my blocking assignment. My job was to block down on him. The technique, as we were taught, was to put my nose on his hip and drive, opening a hole off tackle where the running back could go.

As we lined up, I noticed that he had a grass stain on his hip – at precisely the point where my nose needed to be. When I got into my stance and waited while the quarterback called the cadence, I locked in – I focused on that grass stain. When the ball was snapped, I did what I was taught. I put my nose on that grass stain and started to drive. Ultimately, our feet became tangled and we fell.

When I looked up, I was face to face with our center. I had driven that defender across the tackle spot, across the guard spot, all the way to the center of the line. I can't begin to tell you the satisfaction I got from that.

It was my focusing on that innocuous grass stain that allowed me to carry out my assignment.

By the way, our running back scored from the five-yard line on the play.

Epilogue

I've covered at length, how lessons learned while playing football can have practical applications in the world of business. These lessons, however, also can extend well beyond business – to the very core of life itself. Yes Virginia, there even are football lessons that can be applied directly to life.

A few years ago I had lunch with a former teammate. We reminisced a lot and talked about a lot of different things. One subject he brought up was my wife's passing. She struggled for 4½ years with breast cancer before she finally succumbed. That, too, is another story for another day.

I think it's safe to say however that, after her diagnosis, our lives pretty much revolved around her illness. Doctor visits. Medications. Surgeries. Chemotherapy. Radiation. Hair loss… and the wigs! Oh, the wigs. All that and more. The whole nine yards.

Dealing with it all wasn't easy. It was notably difficult because our daughter was only 10 and was finishing the fourth grade when my wife first was diagnosed. It was a tough time. Just as our daughter was starting high school, my wife turned for the worse and passed away two months after our daughter's 14th birthday.

The last few months were especially difficult. In between the standard routine of doctors, visits, therapies and the like, there were home health aides, home visits and the Sunday nights spent calling friends and family planning for round-the-clock coverage during the week. Then, there were the drugs, the meals, the feedings, the cleanings, the changings, the late nights, the middles of the night, the shopping, the lawn, the laundry; being a Dad, etc. I'm not going to lie to you, it wasn't fun.

Back to my lunch meeting. When Tom, my former teammate, commented on how tough dealing with all that must have been, he wondered out loud, "How did you ever do it?"

Without thinking and without so much as looking up from my lunch, I simply shrugged and said, "Well, you know. You just do what you have to do."

Then it suddenly hit me. The light bulb went on over my head. I looked at him and said, "Tom, isn't that what they taught us in football? 'You do what you have to do.' When you have third and one, you don't think about it. You just go out and get that yard to make your first down and keep the ball. You don't think about it. You just do it." You do what you have to do. (With no apologies to Nike, I didn't steal their tagline, I lived it.) And that is precisely what they taught us in football. When faced with any kind of a challenge, you just go out and do what you have to do.

My wife needed to be cared for. There was no other option. I did what I had to do. My daughter did what she had to do. In the end, it wasn't easy but we got through it. Of course, my wife did what she had to do too – she fought tooth and nail for 4½ years. Make no mistake, she took that game all the way into the fourth quarter. Unfortunately, her opponent was bigger and stronger. But that didn't diminish her effort – or the efforts of the many friends, family and acquaintances who also helped and were there for her when she needed them.

Although we lost that game, it wasn't for lack of trying.

Life. Business. Football. Yeah, when you get right down to it, they're all pretty much one and the same. And maybe that's the way it should be.

Made in the USA
Monee, IL
27 September 2022